THIS

SIMPLY SATISFYING

COLORING BOOK BELONGS TO:

_____

RECOMMENDED MEDIA: COLORED PENCILS & CRAYONS

If you do intend to use markers or other oil, water or alcohol based mediums,
it is best to place a sheet of card stock in between the pages to prevent
any bleed through to the next page.

SPECIAL THANK YOU!

I would like to say thank you for choosing this
Simply Satisfying Large Print Coloring Book
and supporting my small business!
If you are enjoying these minimalistic designs, **please leave a review**
as your feedback will help Diddy's Designs continue to grow and produce
high quality content for many books to come.

MORE GREAT BOOKS

For more great experiences,
scan the QR code to check out some of
my other activity books for creative
enthusiasts of all ages!

Simply Satisfying Large Print Coloring Book - Winter Edition
Published by Bailey Braden @ Diddy's Designs © 2023

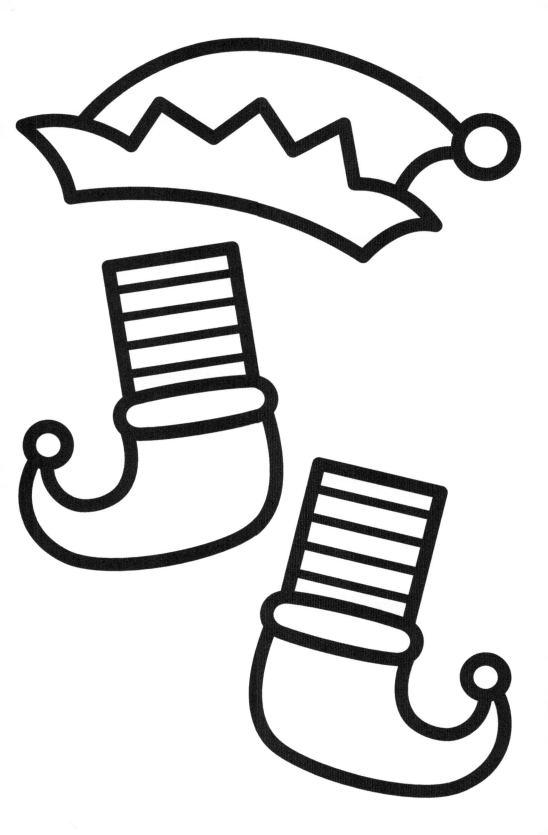

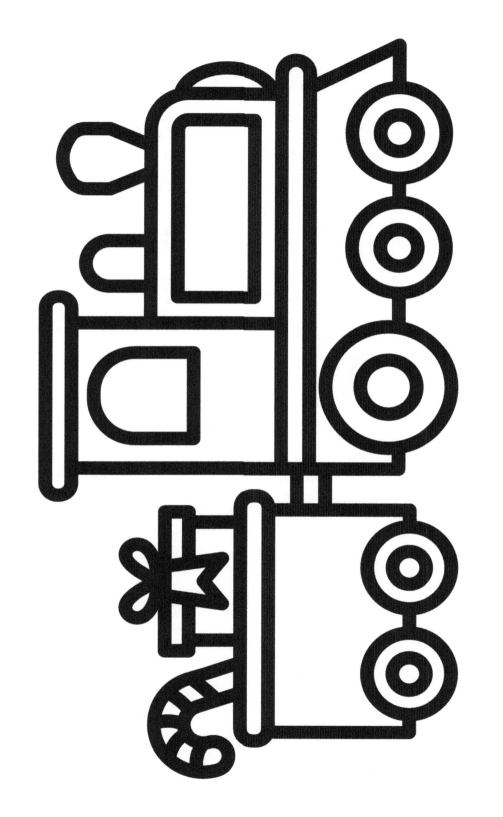

Made in the USA
Middletown, DE
28 November 2024

65587107R00071